HOW DUBLIN BUSKER BROUGHT GOOD LUCK TO DUBLIN

Published by Simona's Library

For more information about this book or to contact the author, please visit

www.simonaslibrary.com

Printed and bound in England.

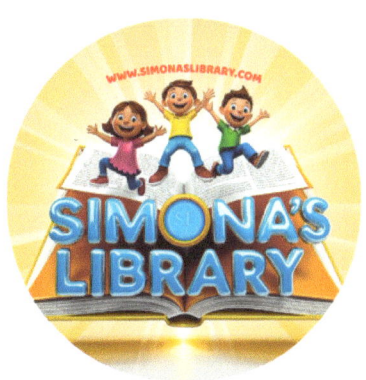

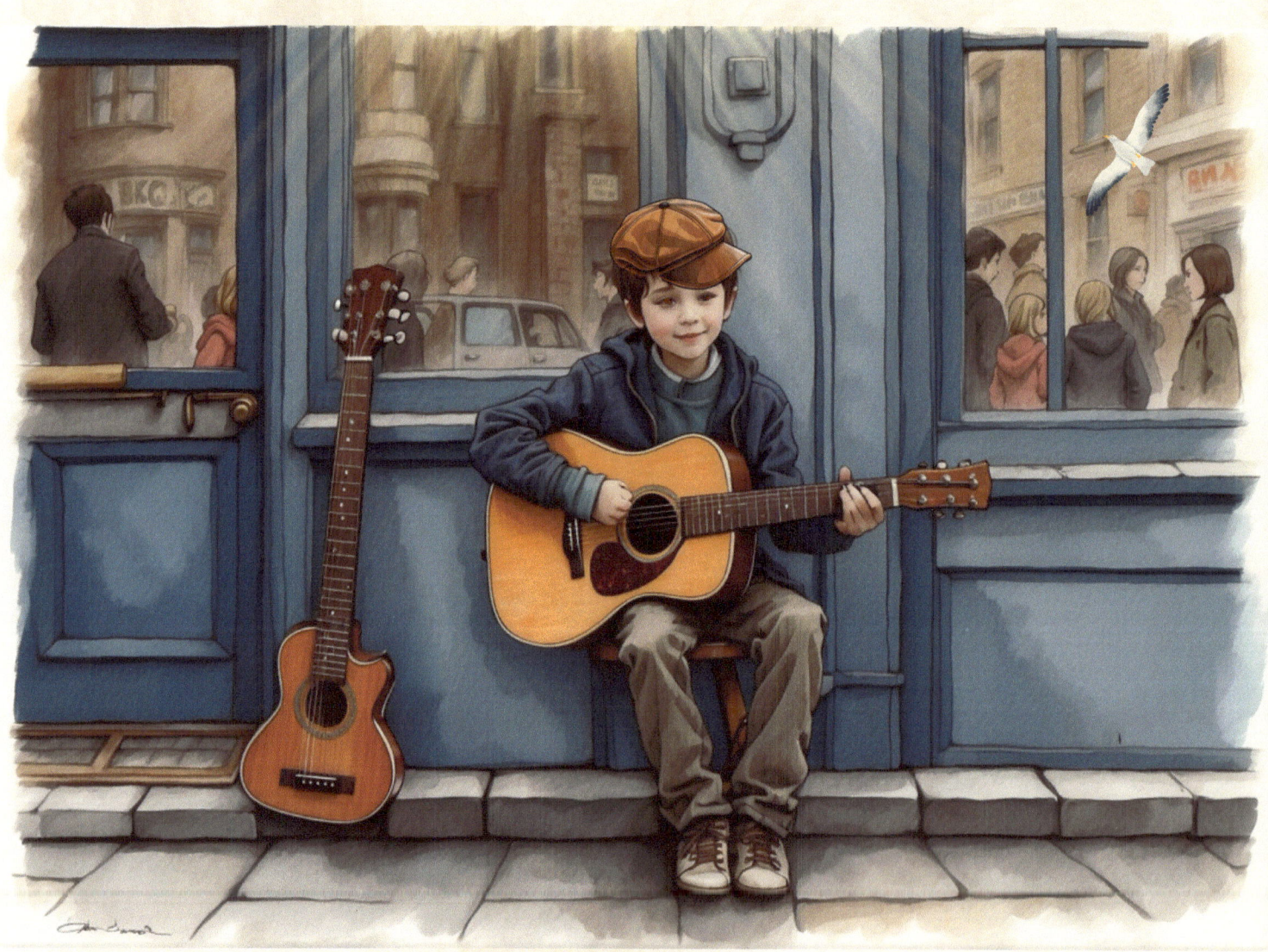

This book belongs to:

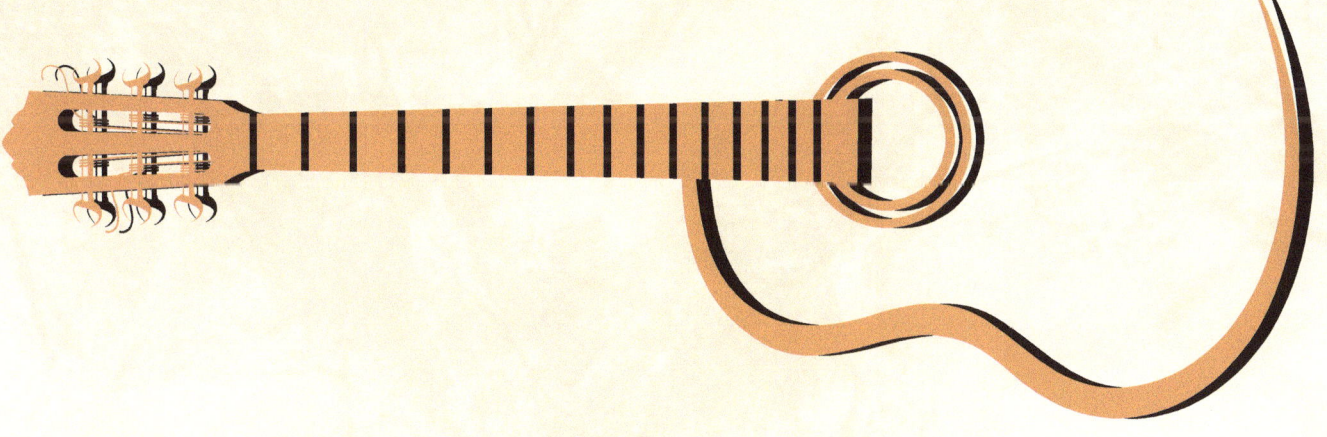

Scan the QR code to listen to the story

In the magical city of Dublin, lived a kind-hearted busker named Liam. Every day, he played his guitar on the bustling streets, filling the air with beautiful melodies that touched everyone's heart.

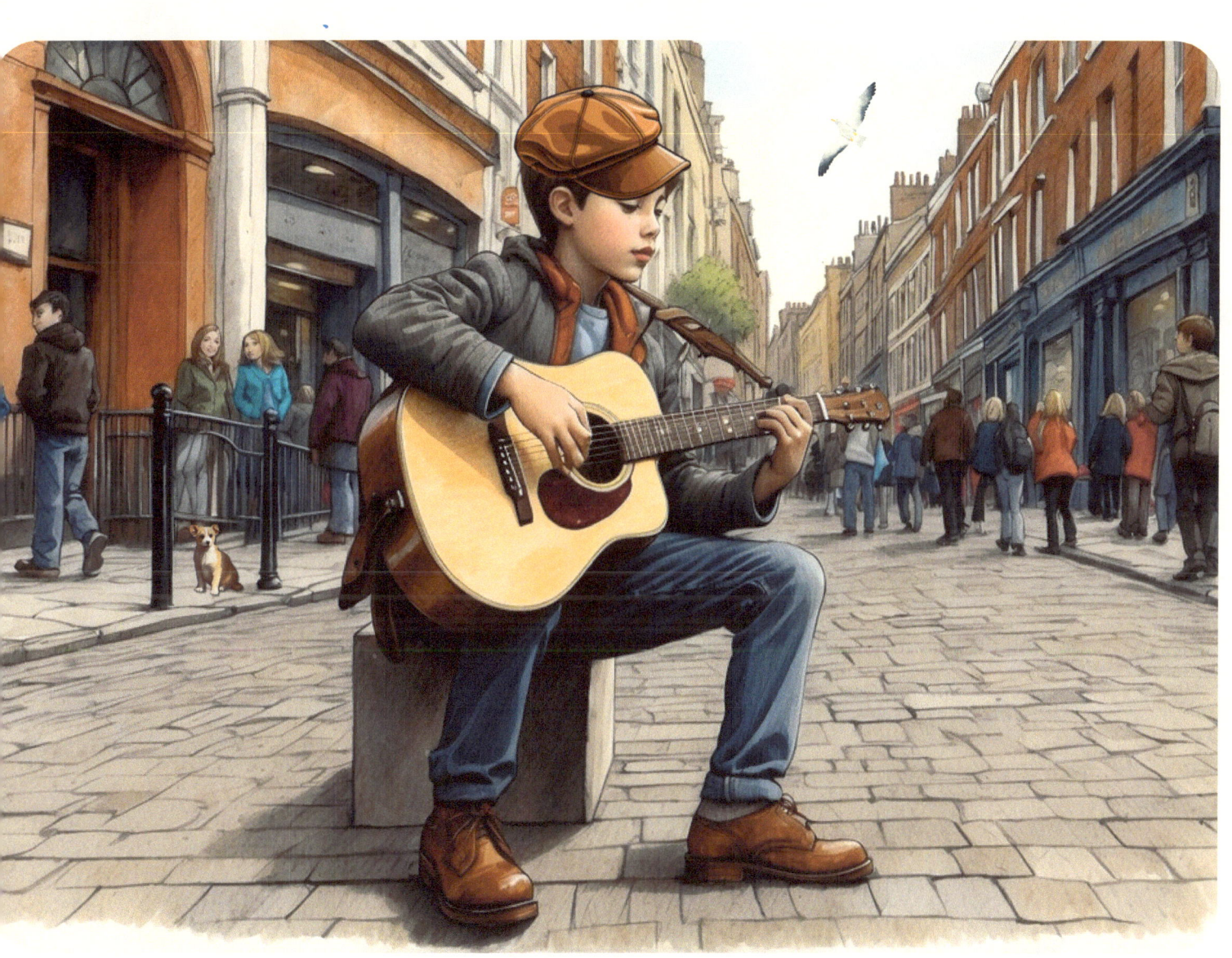

One sunny morning, Liam stumbled upon a small, shiny penny lying near his guitar case. Little did he know that this simple coin held extraordinary powers. As soon as Liam picked up the penny, his luck began to change.

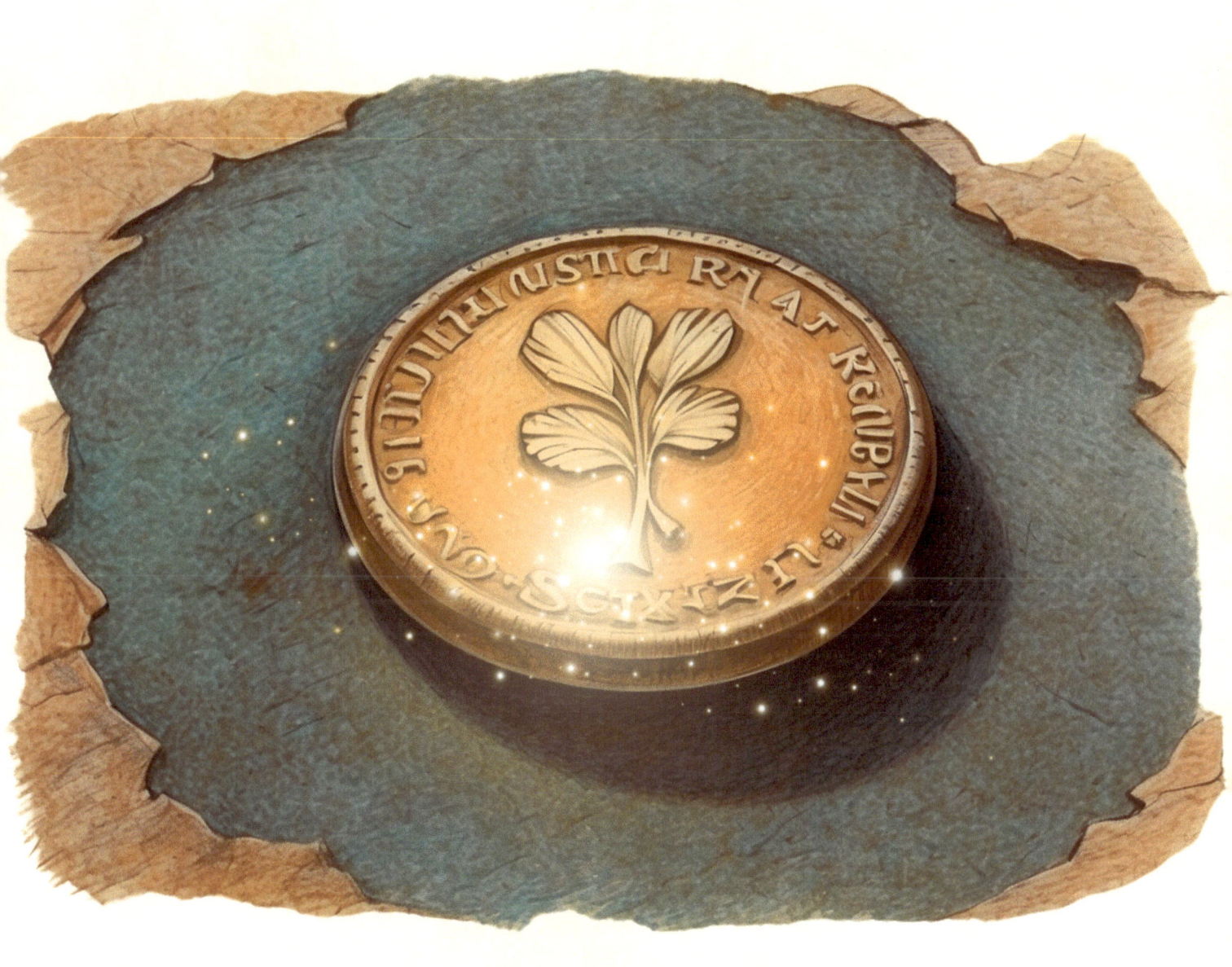

Each day, the sun shone just a little brighter, and the people of Dublin became happier. They couldn't resist dancing and smiling as Liam played his enchanting tunes. Dublin became a city brimming with joy and laughter.

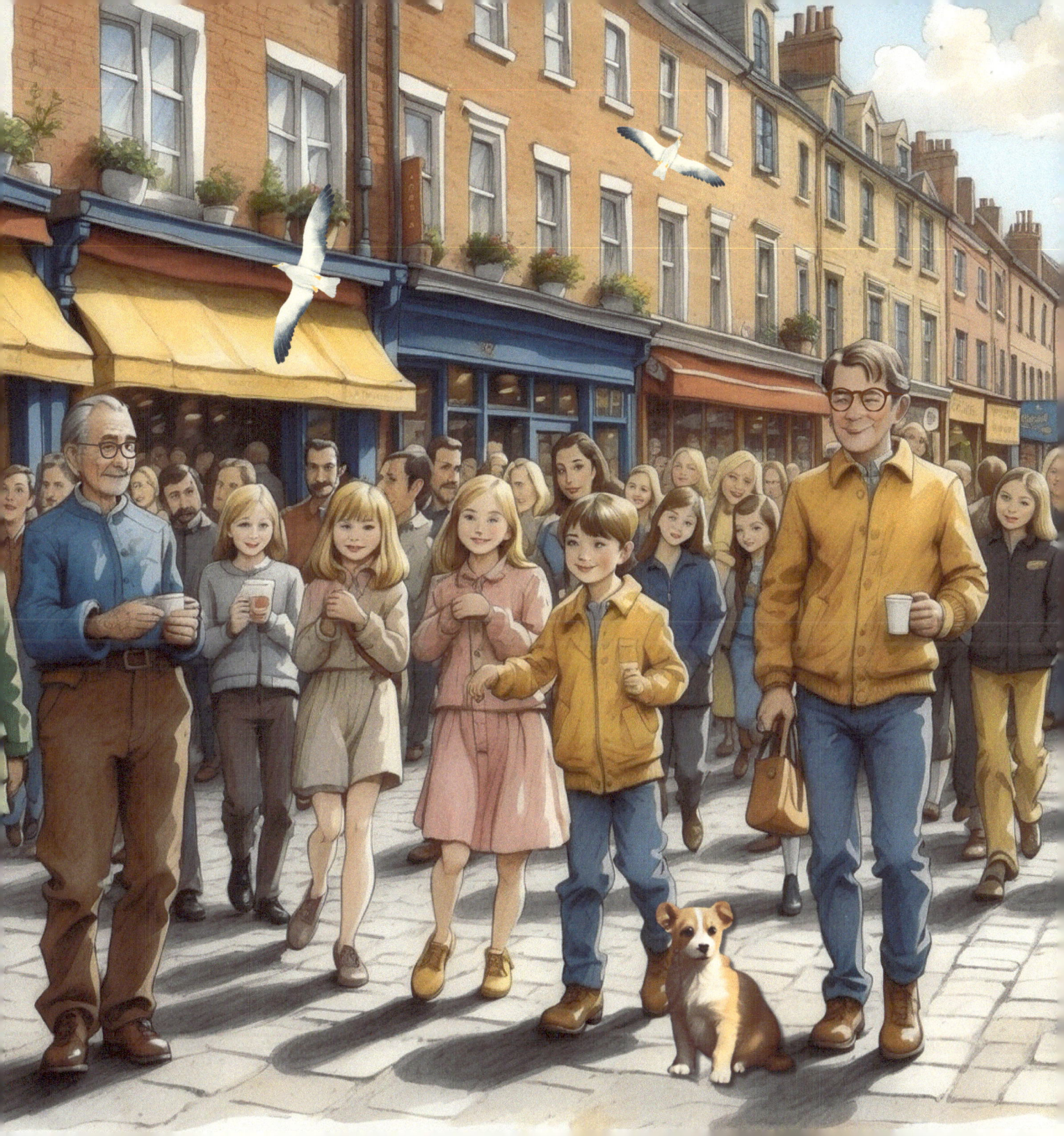

Children would gather around Liam, eyes filled with wonder, as he strummed his guitar and sang cheerful melodies. The sweet sounds seemed to create a magical aura, drawing people together. Even the birds chirped along, creating a beautiful harmony that echoed throughout the city.

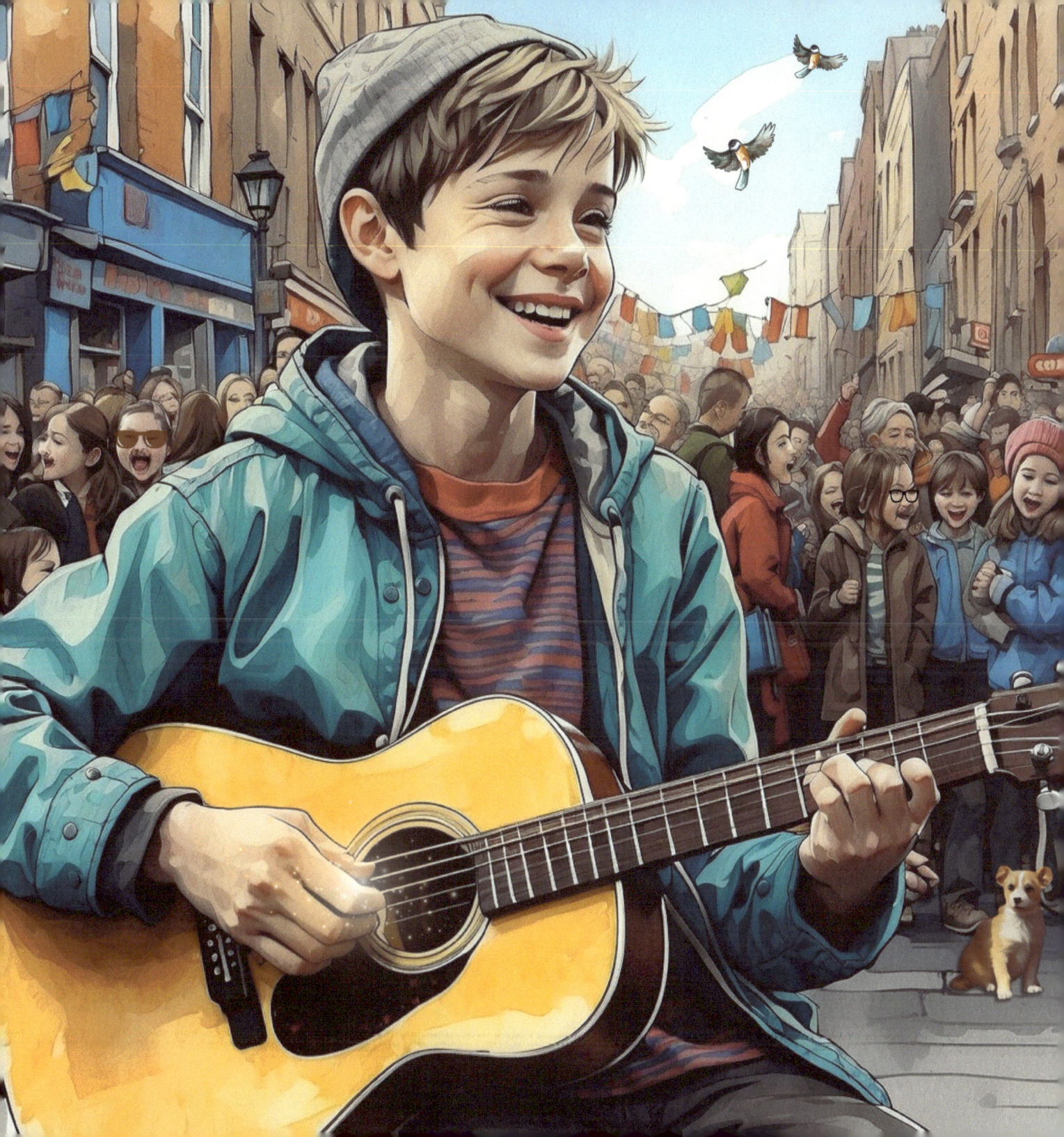

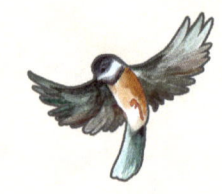

But Liam was not selfish. He knew that his newfound luck had to be shared. So, he decided to perform in hospitals and orphanages, spreading joy to the children who needed it most. His music healed their hearts and brought smiles to their faces.

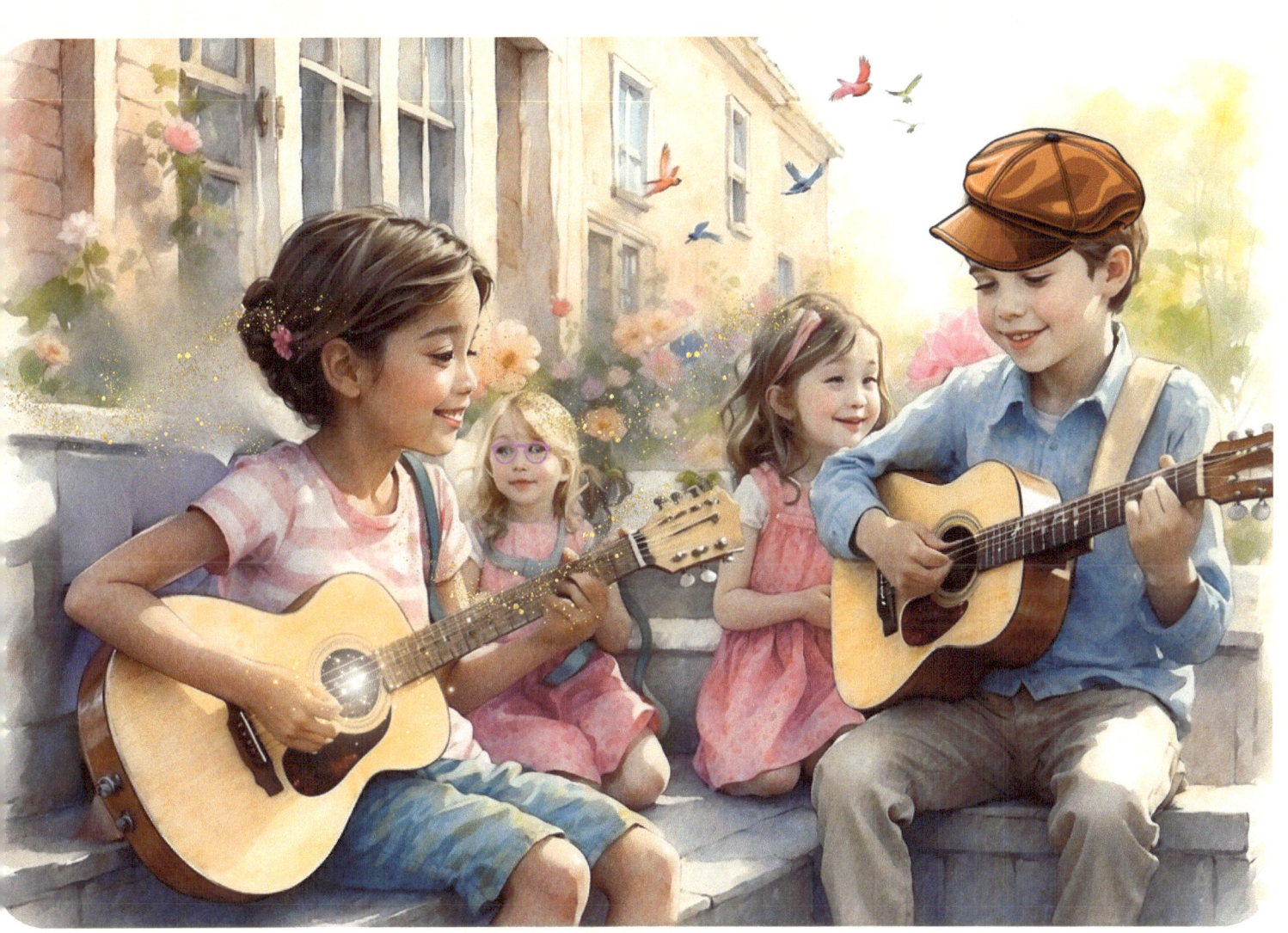

Word of Liam's incredible performances spread far and wide, and people from all around the world flocked to Dublin just to listen to him play. With each note he played, the city grew even luckier, and Dublin became known as the "City of Joy."

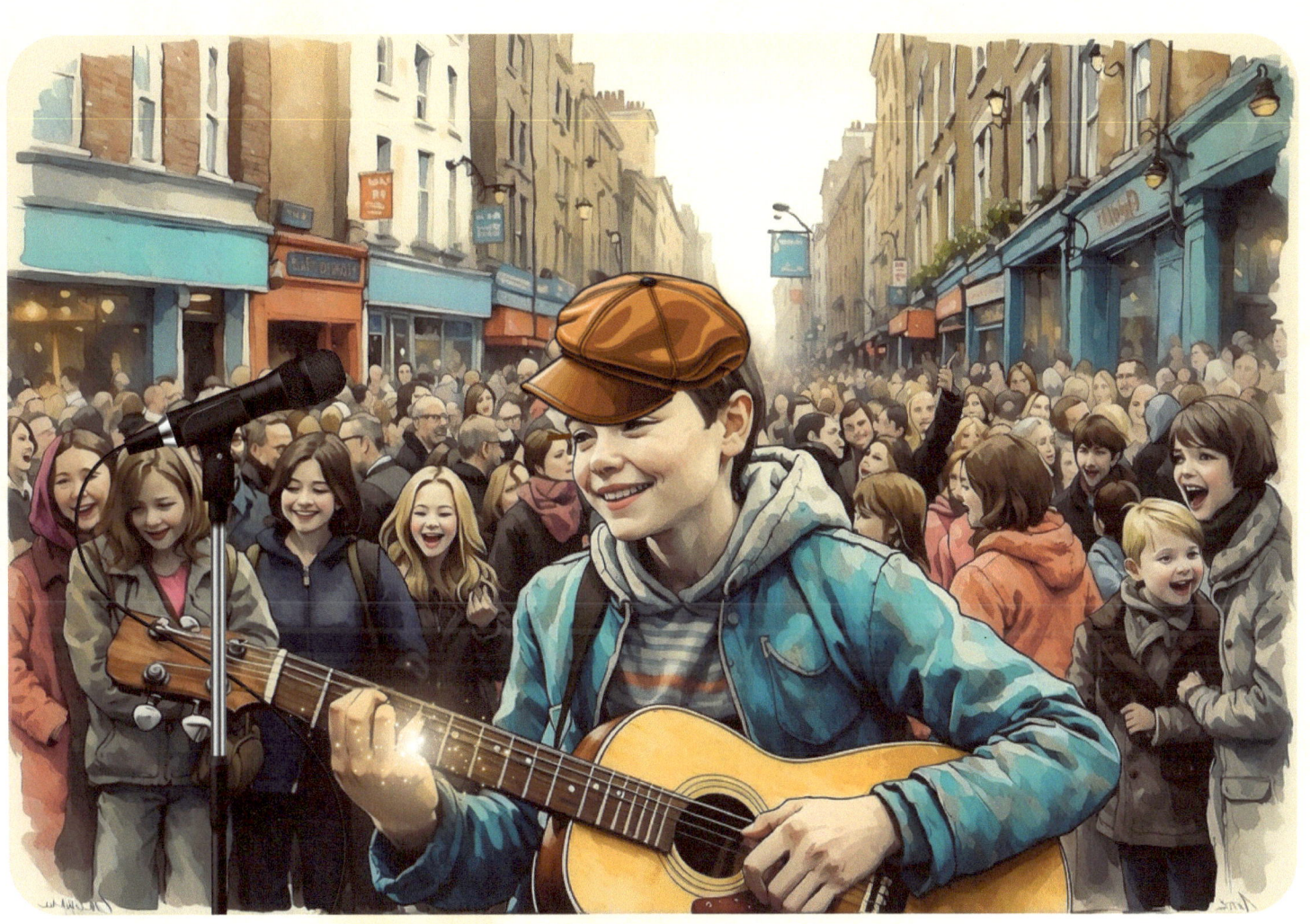

One day, as Liam played his guitar in the park, a lonely and disheartened old man sat on a nearby bench. The man had lost all hope and couldn't remember the last time he had smiled.

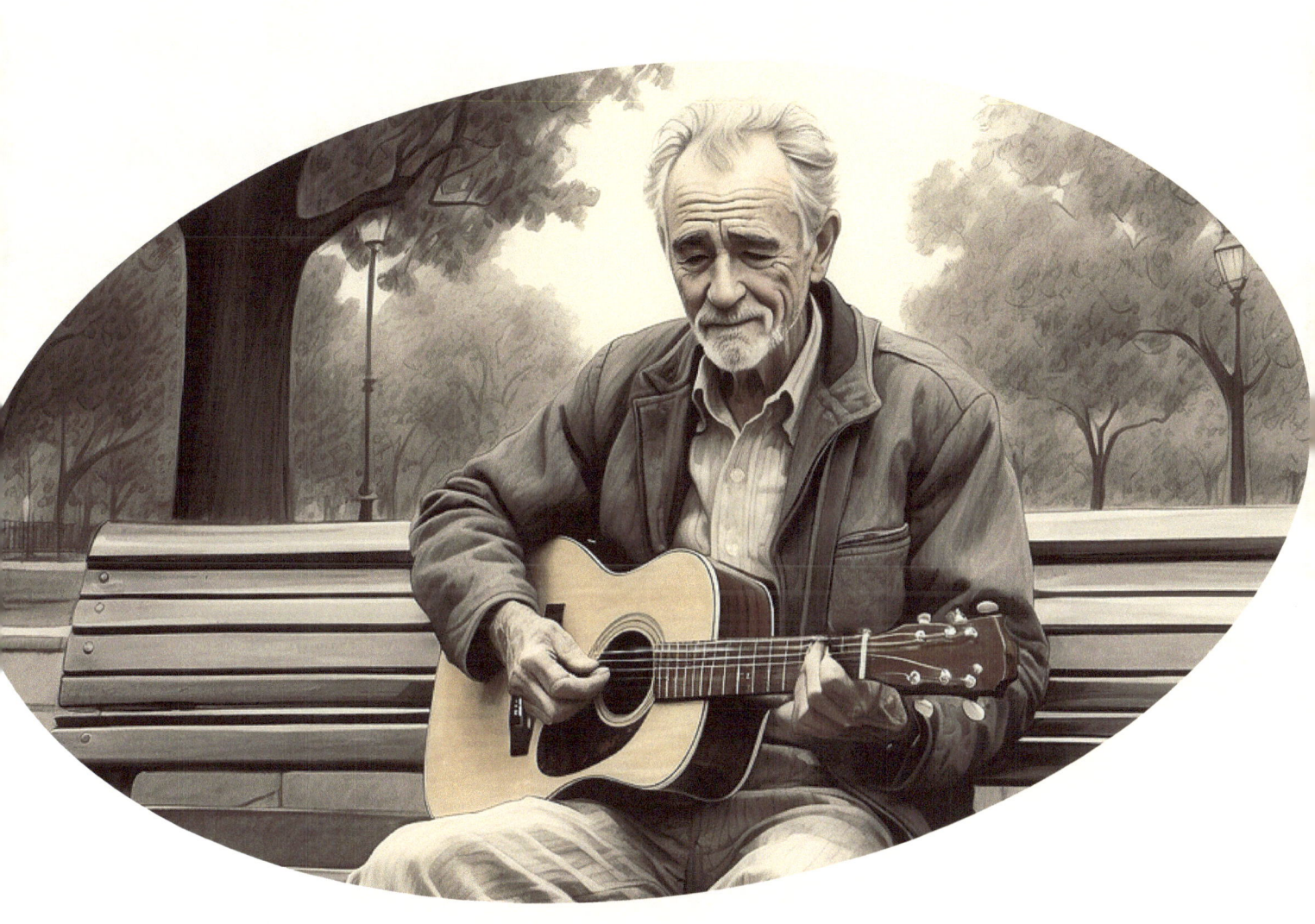

Sensing the man's sadness, Liam approached him and played a soul-stirring melody. The old man's eyes sparkled with happiness, and a wide smile appeared on his face. Dublin's luck had spread to this lonely soul.

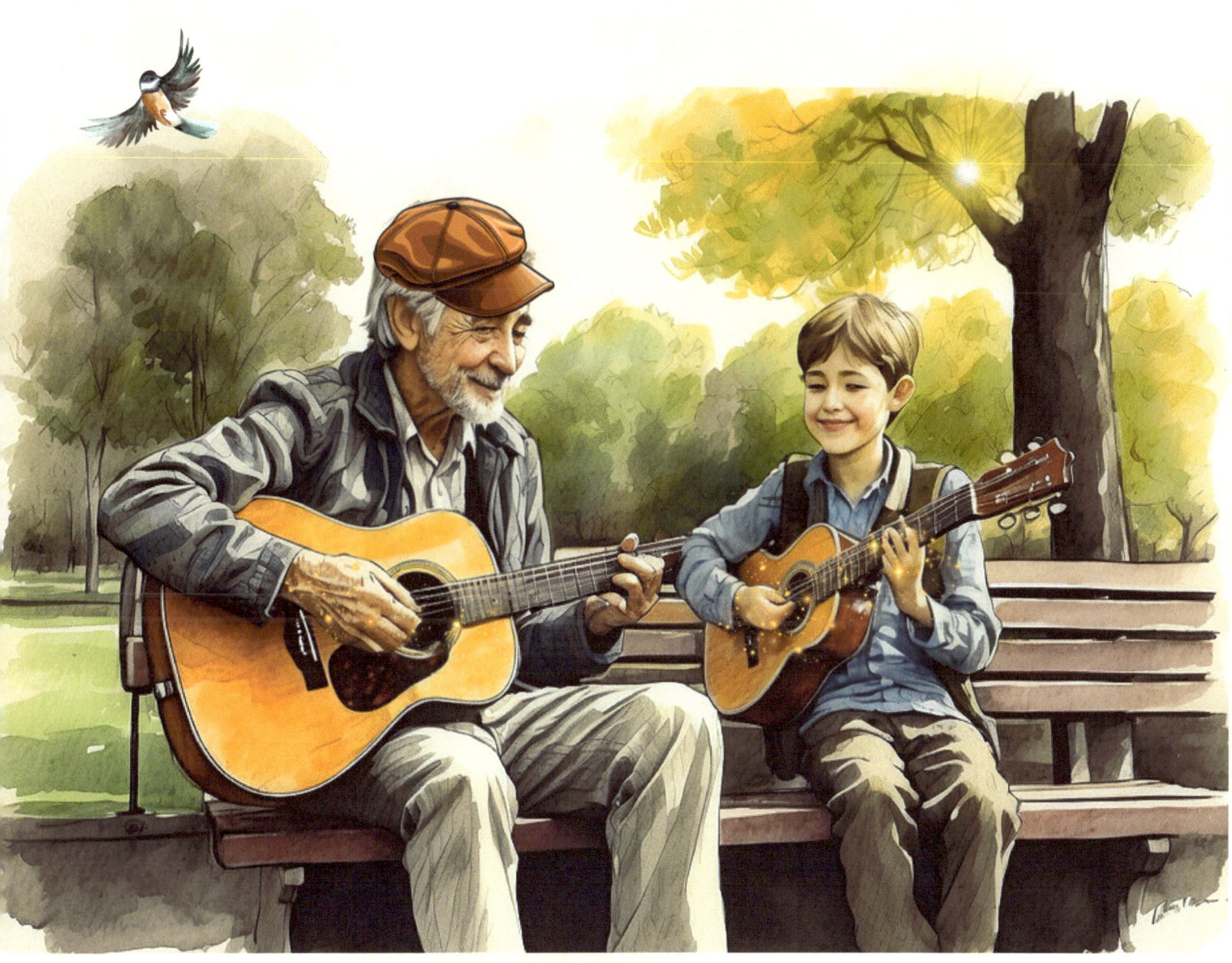

In that very moment, the penny in Liam's pocket glowed brilliantly, lifting into the air and transforming into a shining star.

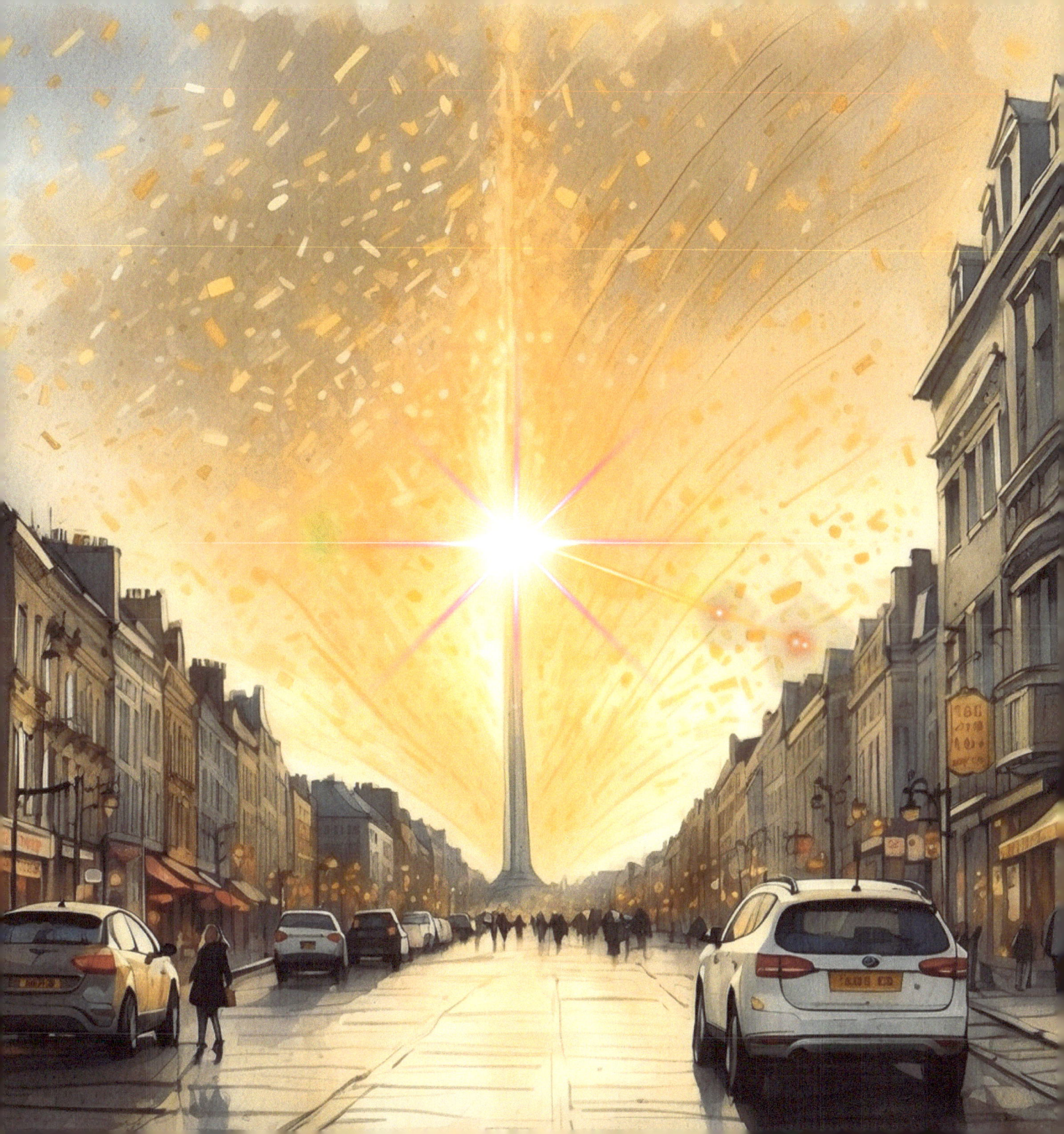

The star showered the entire city with a golden light, embedding the indescribable feeling of joy deep into Dublin's heart.

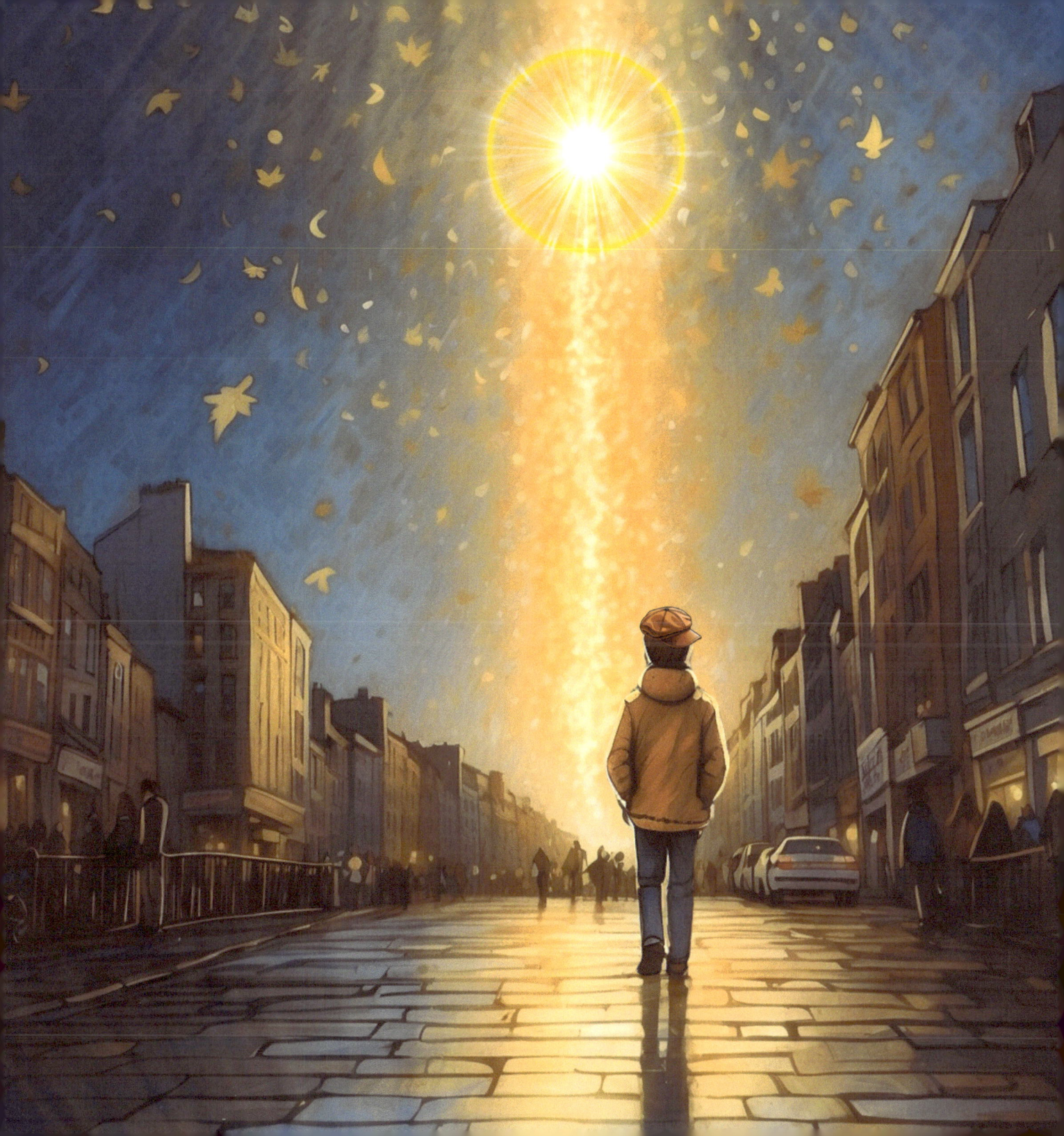

From that day forward, the people of Dublin never forgot the magic that Liam, the busker, brought to their lives.

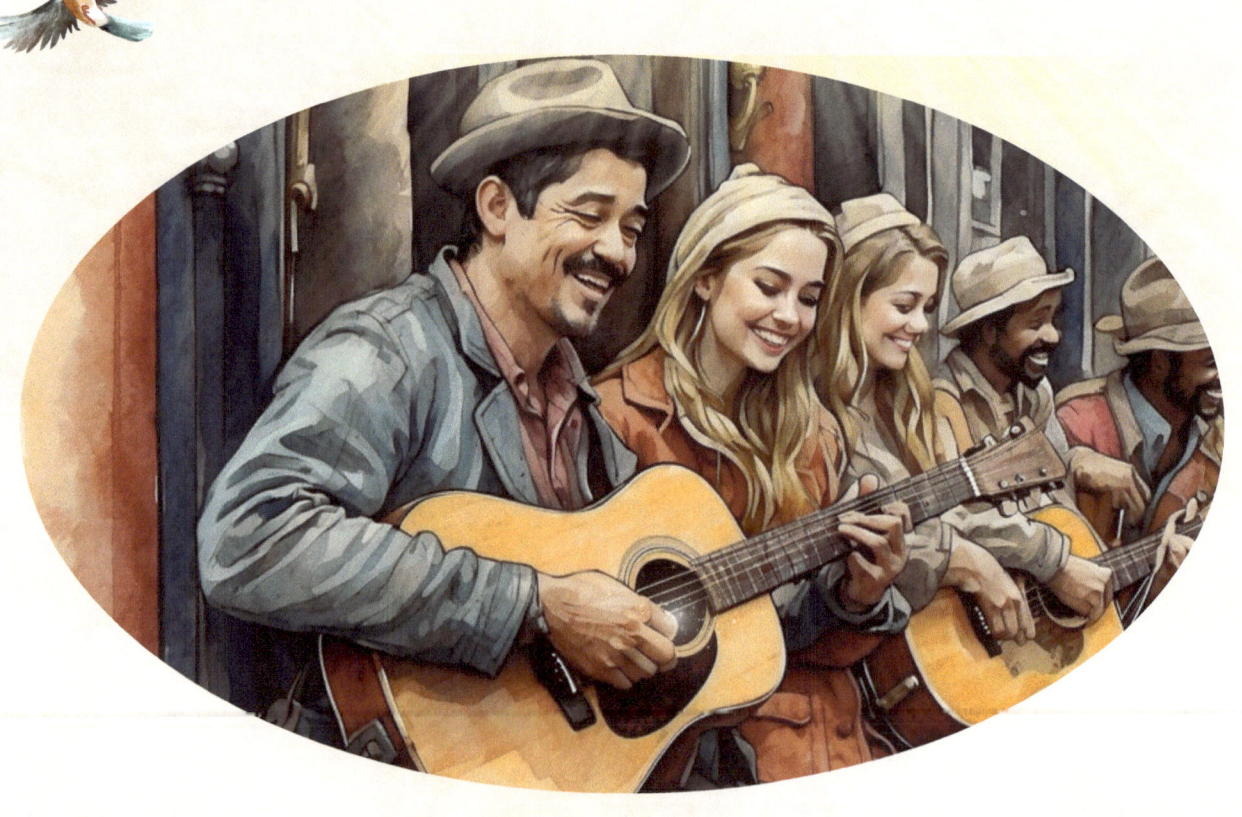

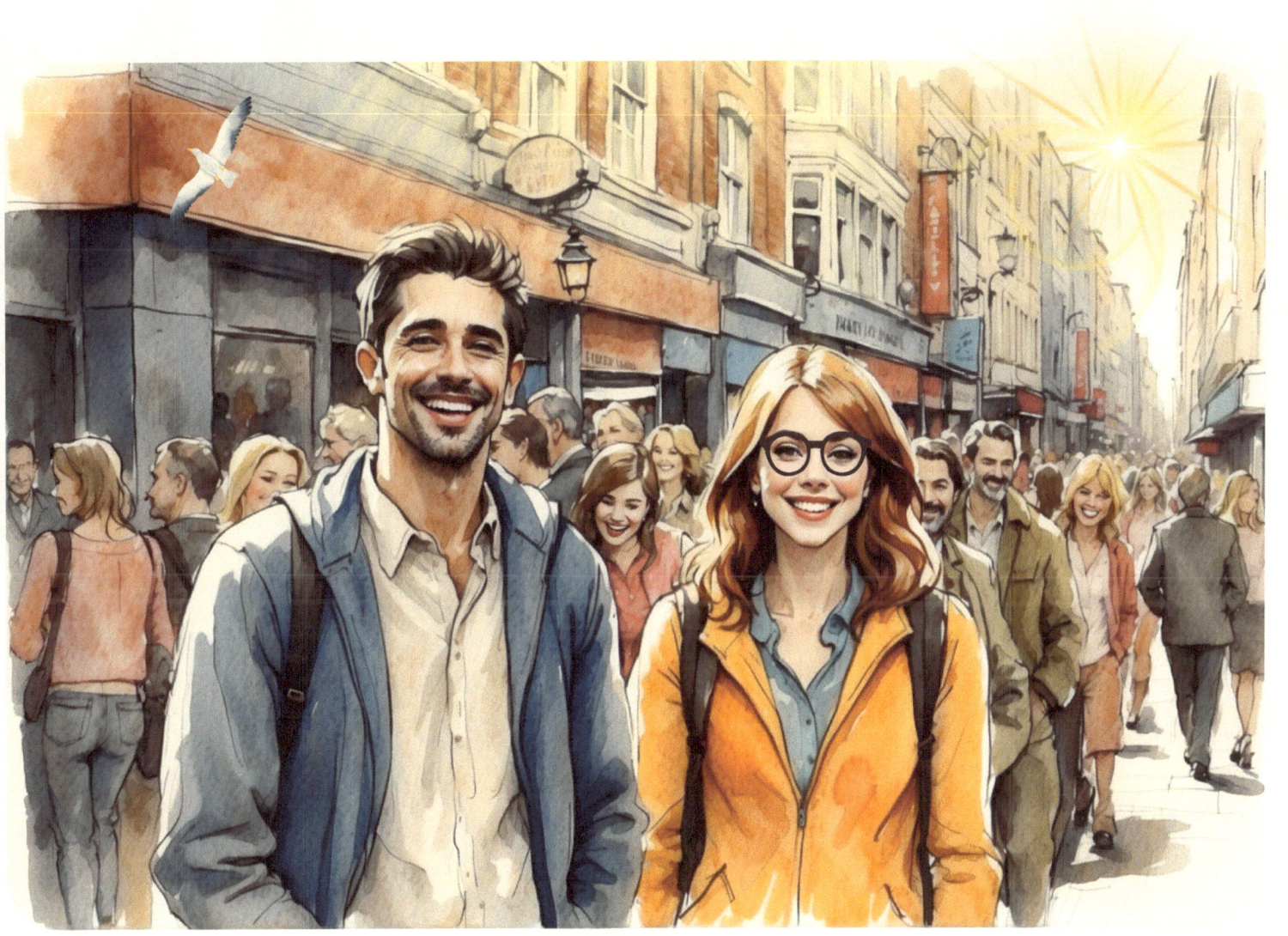

They realized that true happiness lies in sharing and spreading joy with others, just as Liam had done.

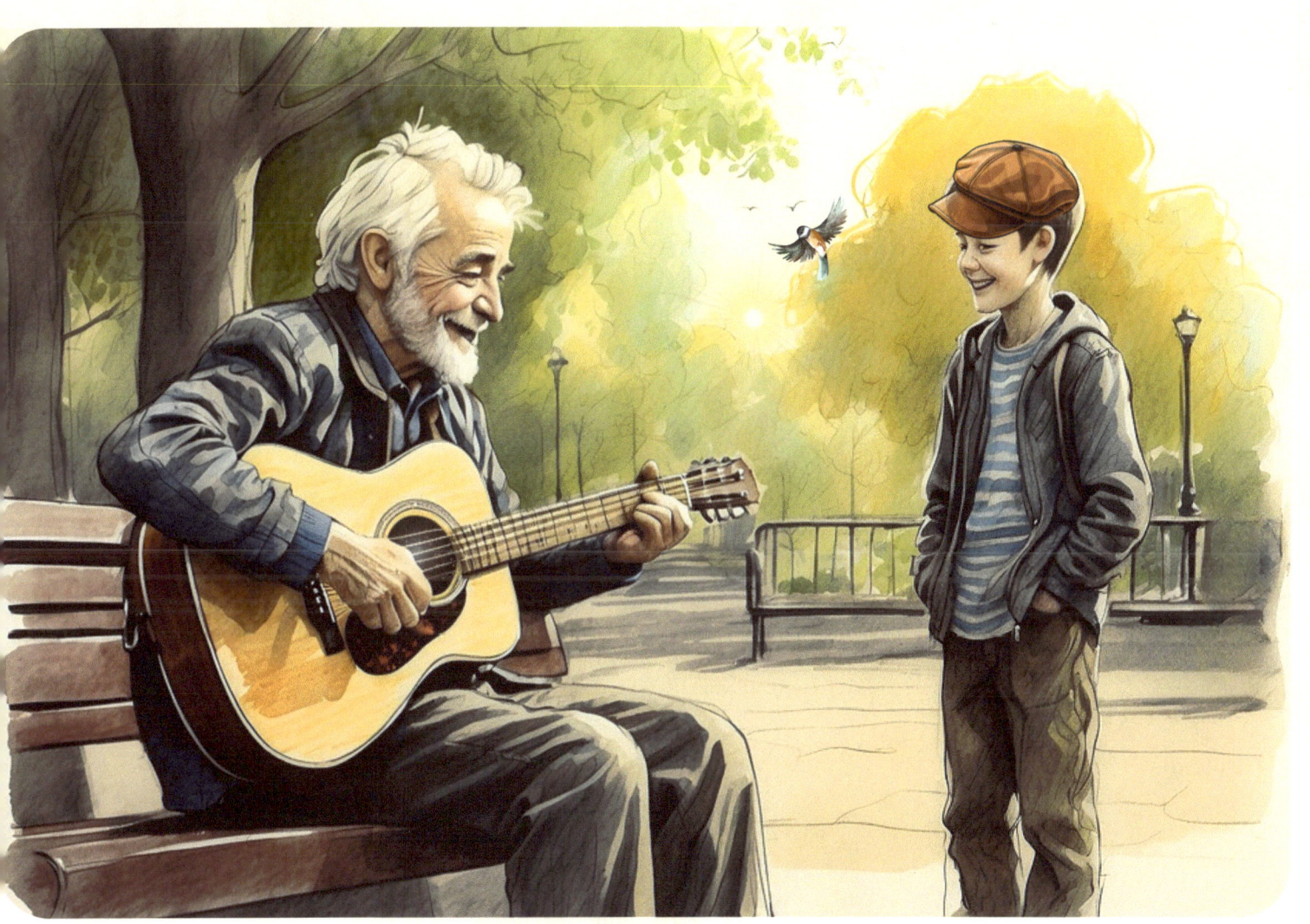

And so, Dublin continued to be a city of music, love, and laughter, all thanks to the humble busker who taught them the true meaning of happiness.

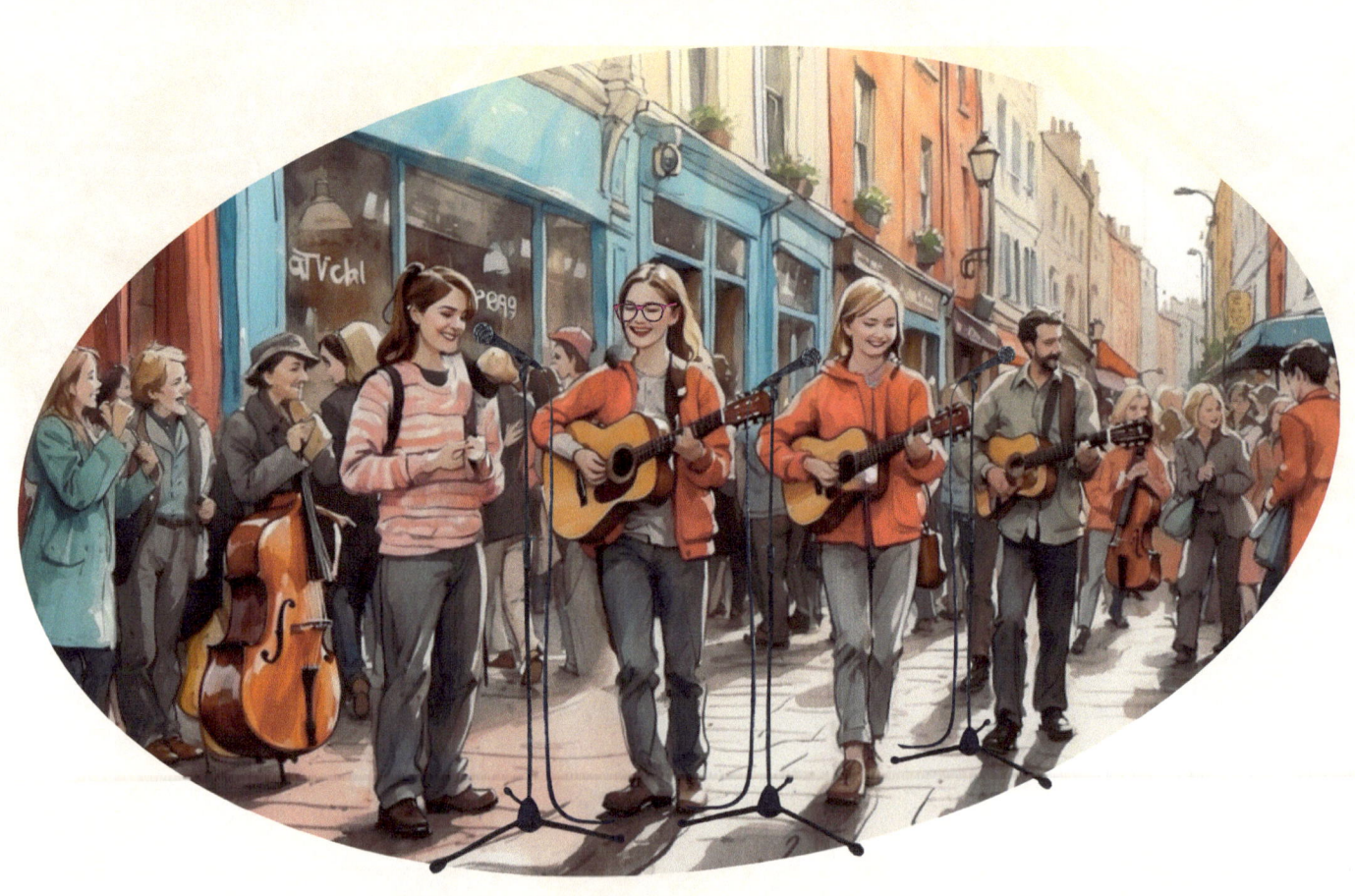

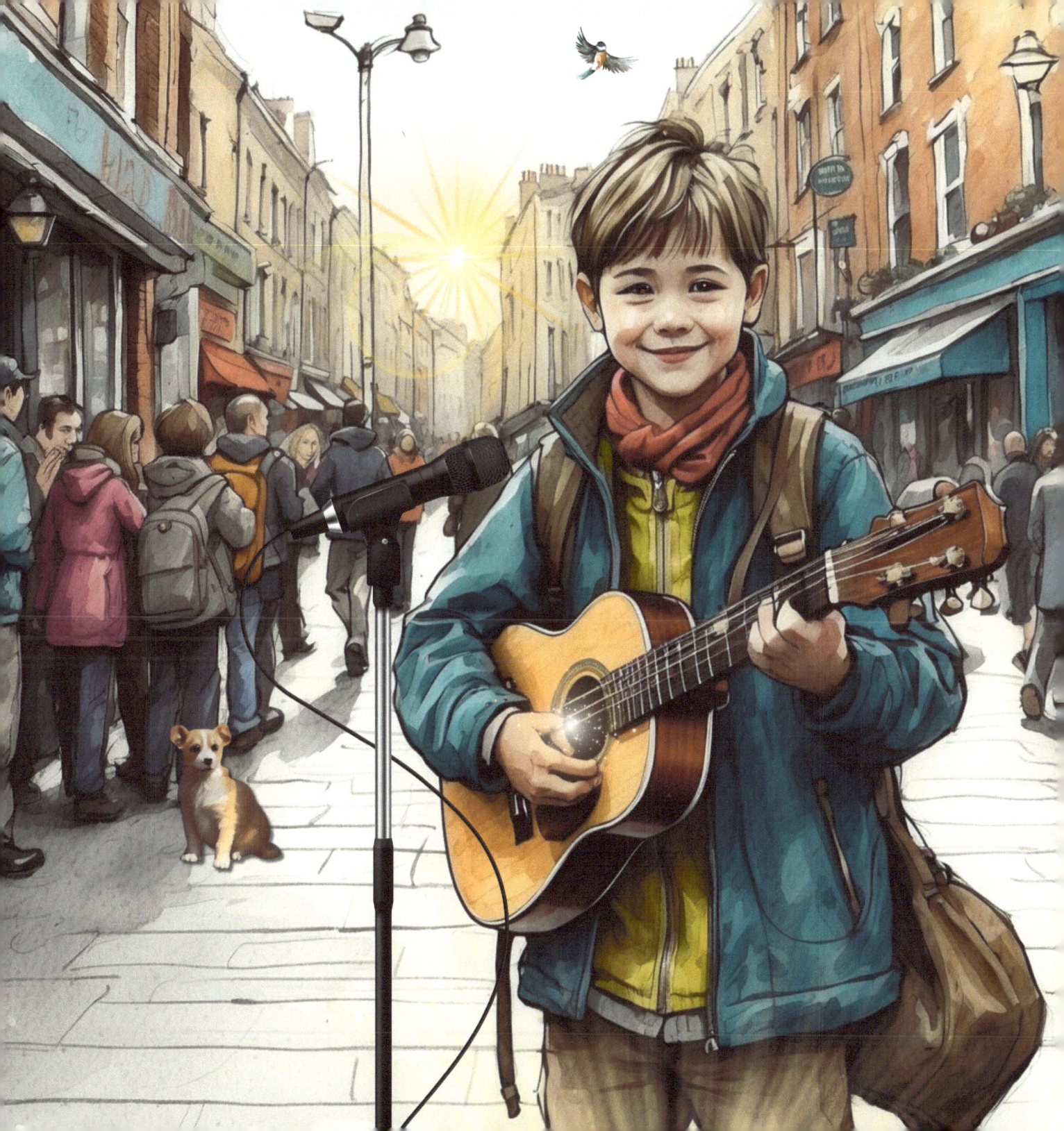

The legacy of Liam's music and the penny's magic
lived on forever, reminding everyone of the power
of bringing joy to others.

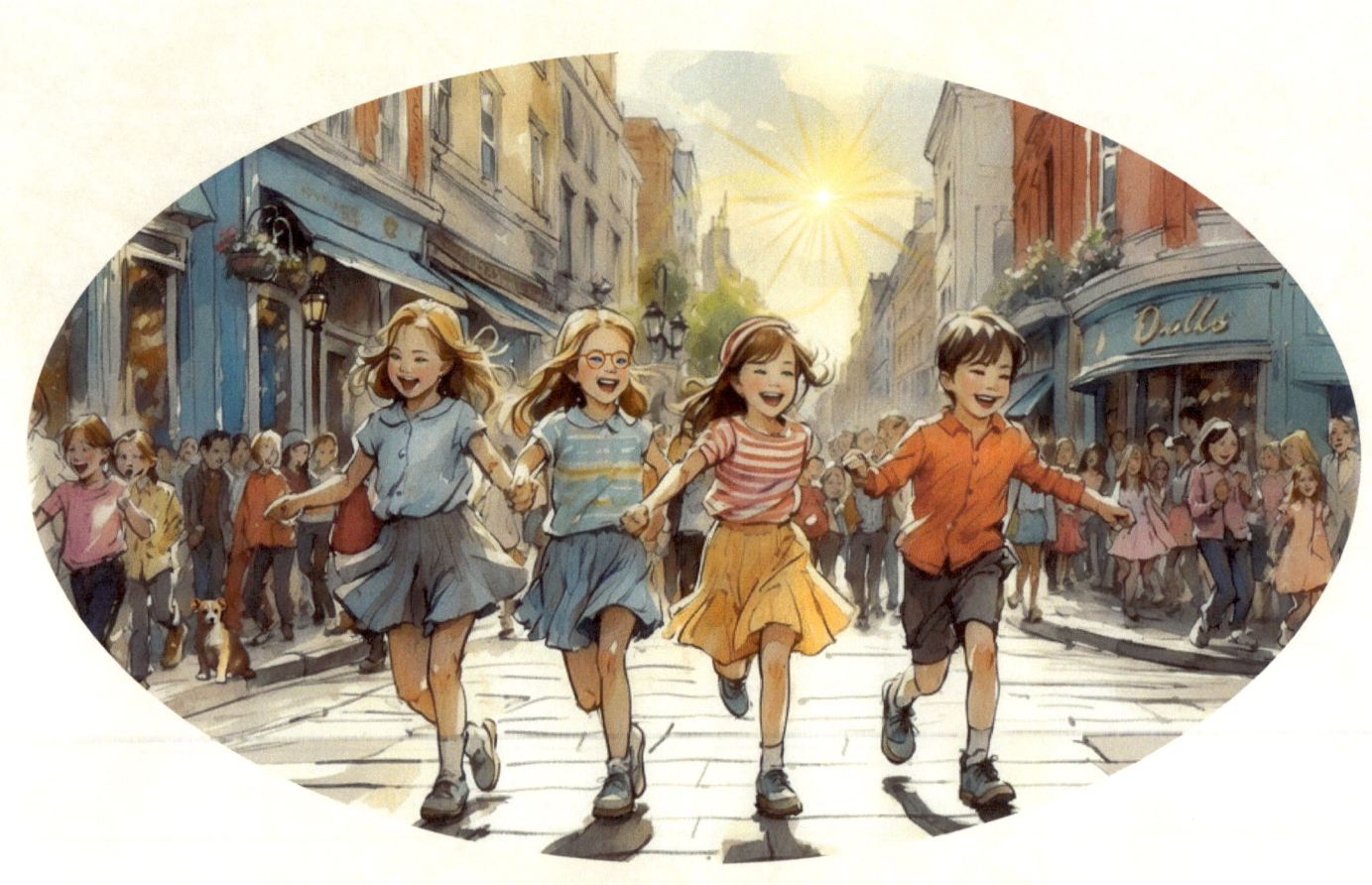

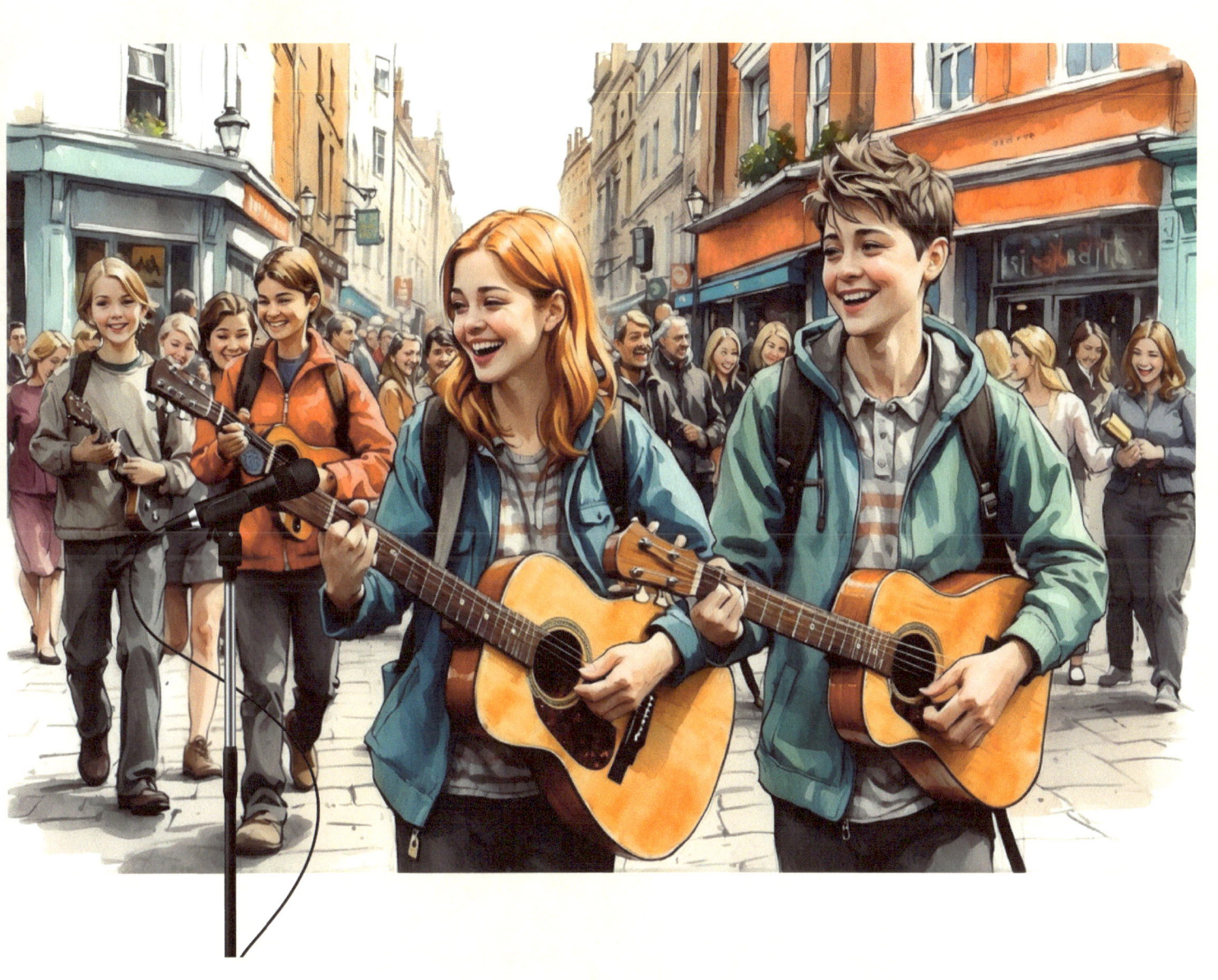

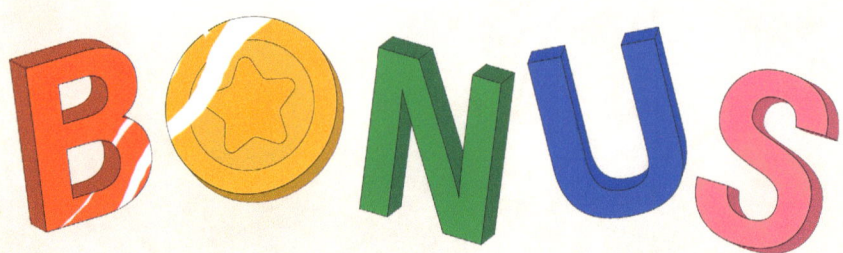

SCAN ME

✨ **Special Bonus!** ✨

Scan the QR code with a phone or tablet and listen to our song made just for you! 🎶💃🕺
Sing, dance, and celebrate along—it's our special gift to you for being part of the story! 🥳🎉

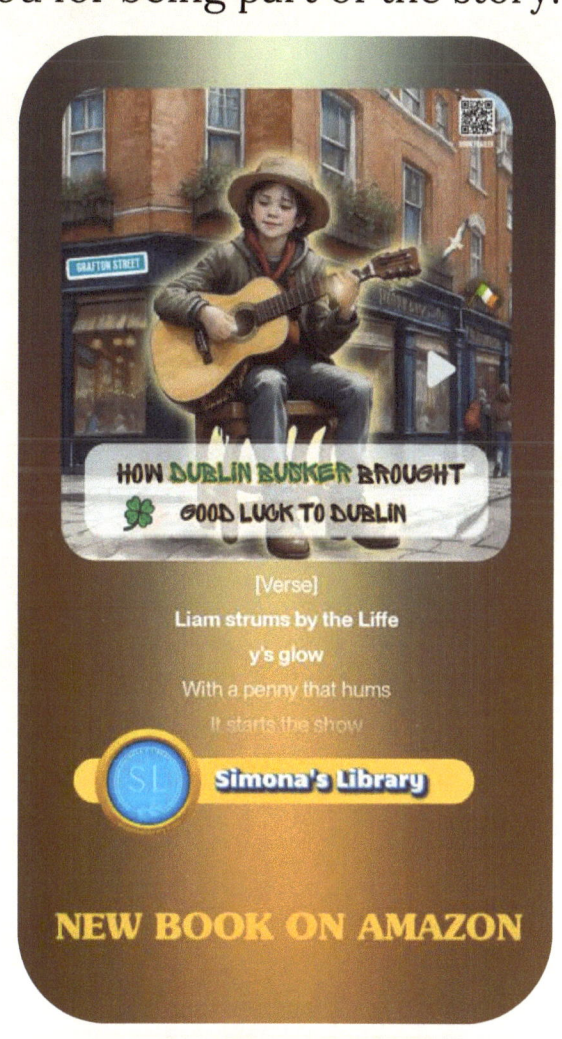

Embark on a melodic journey through the vibrant streets of contemporary Dublin with "Grafton Street Melodies" book, uncovering the soulful tales and captivating tunes of its talented buskers.

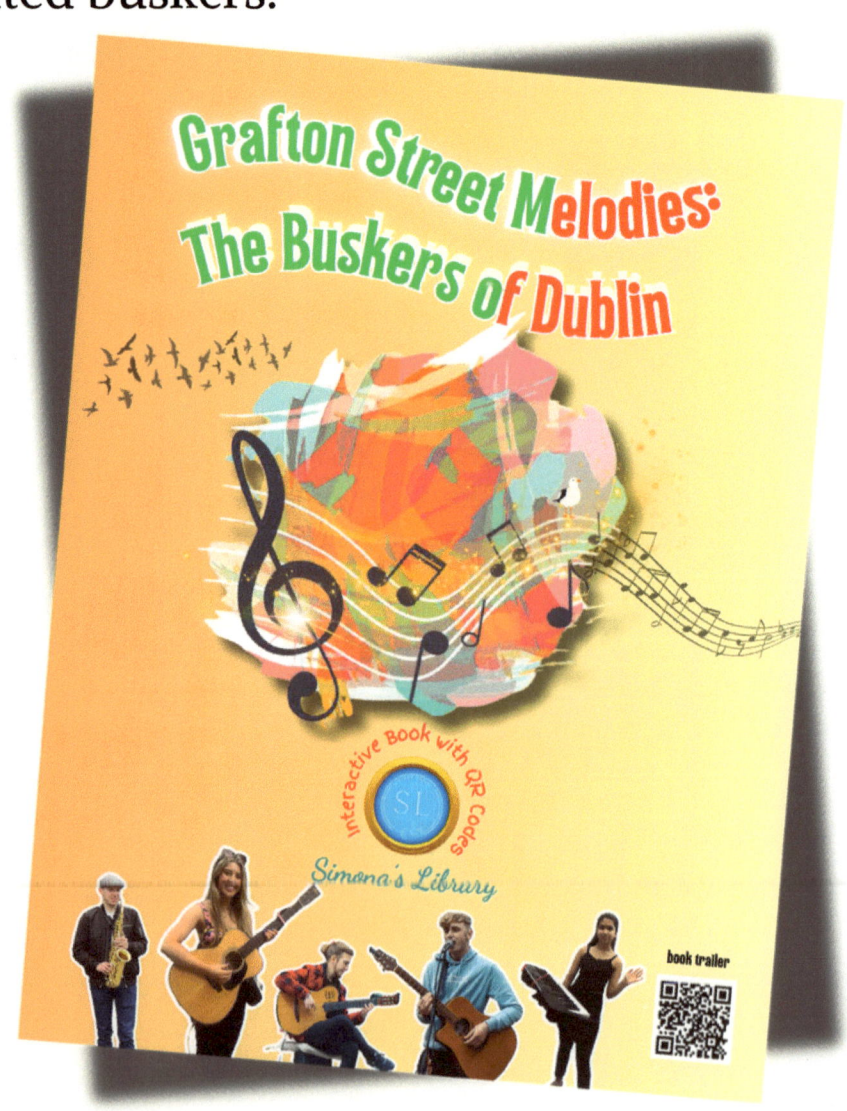

In the book "Grafton Street Melodies: The Buskers of Dublin," (as seen on Forbes) you'll delve into the captivating world of Dublin's buskers. Through insightful interviews and captivating stories, you'll discover the journeys and dreams of these talented individuals, gaining a deeper understanding of their craft and their impact on the city. So, whether you're a tourist, a family, a Dubliner, a shopper, or a buyer, prepare to be enchanted by the melodic tapestry woven by the buskers of Dublin. This book is a tribute to the Dublin buskers and their fans, for together you create a symphony of unity, bridging gaps between strangers, and reminding us of the power of art to unite us all.

Scan here to order:

Book Trailer:

Scan here to visit Simona's Library:

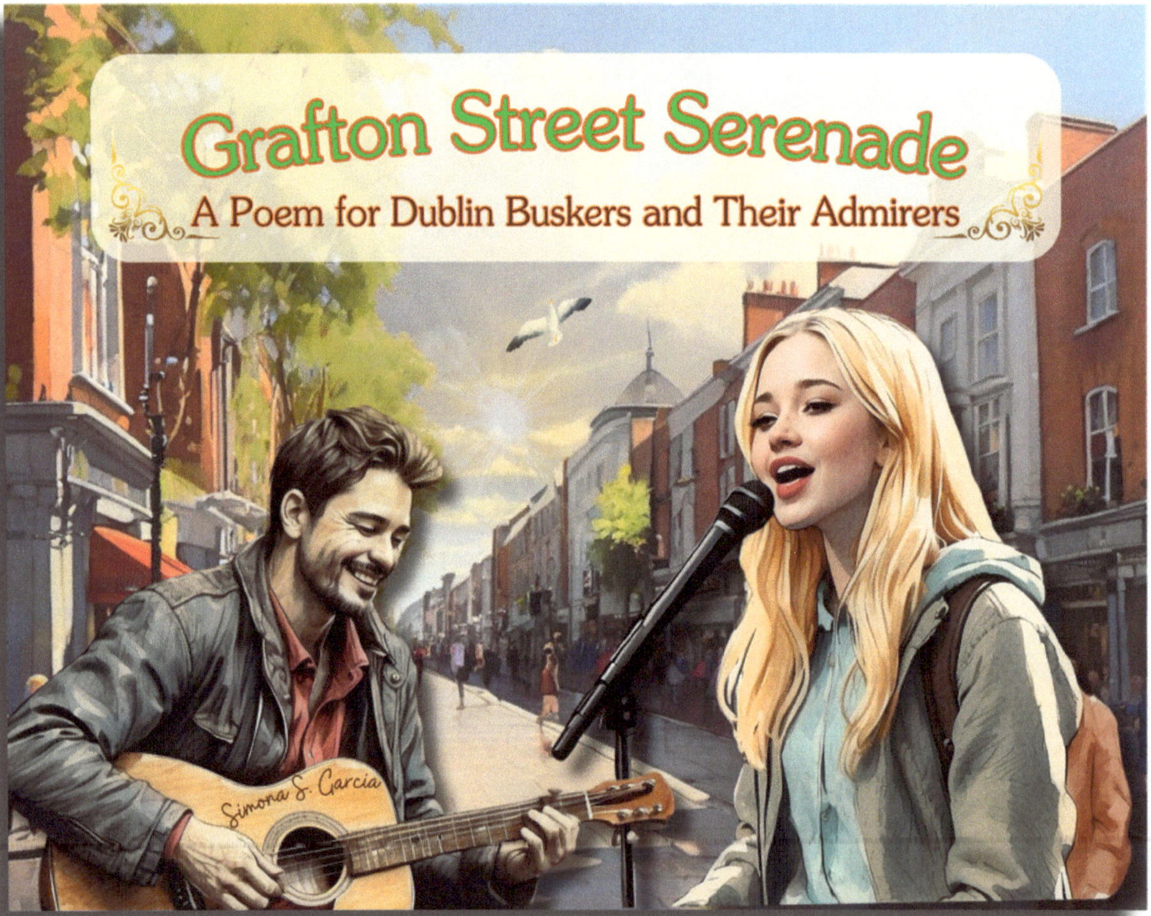

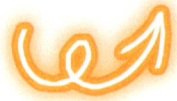 Now on Amazon

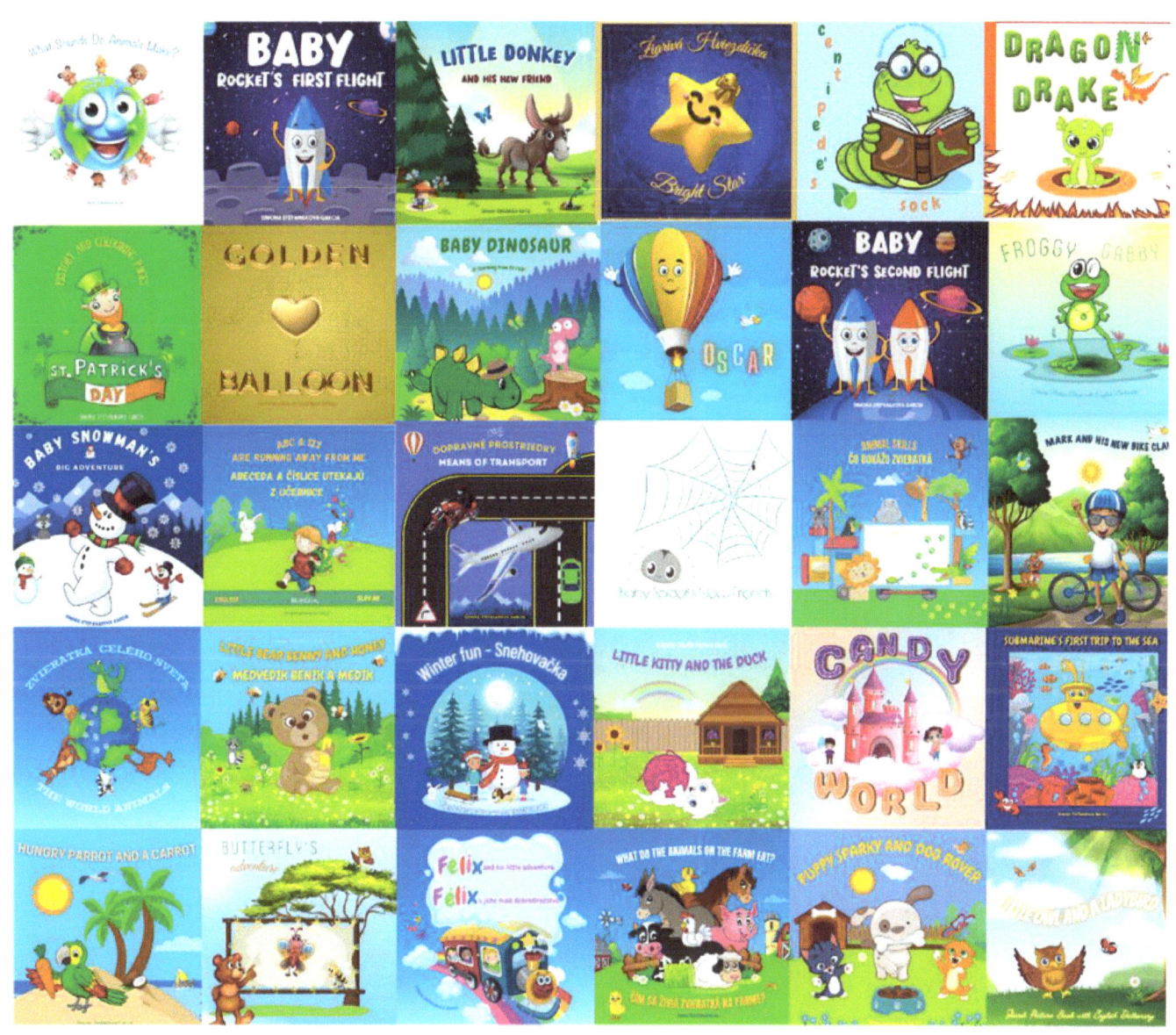

www.simonaslibrary.com

Meet the Author

Simona celebrates stories that empower children to be kind, confident, and courageous. Her books are filled with heart, humor, and meaningful lessons that grow with every reader.

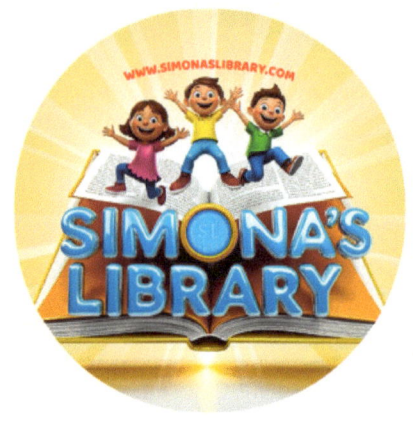

WWW.SIMONASLIBRARY.COM

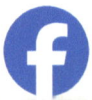    

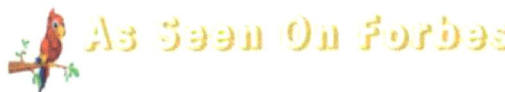 ## As Seen On Forbes

Simona's Library, her brand, encompasses a collection of children's books, bilingual stories, coloring pages, and notebooks designed to inspire and educate children entertainingly. With over 60 published books, numerous notable career highlights, and a robust online presence, Simona is making a significant impact on children's literature and the creative industry.

Simona Stefanakova Garcia, the driving force behind Simona's Library, is a talented and multifaceted creative whose books and videos have enriched the lives of children and families worldwide. Through her captivating stories, innovative illustrations, and engaging videos, Simona continues to inspire young minds and foster a love for reading, learning, and creativity.

View More On Forbes

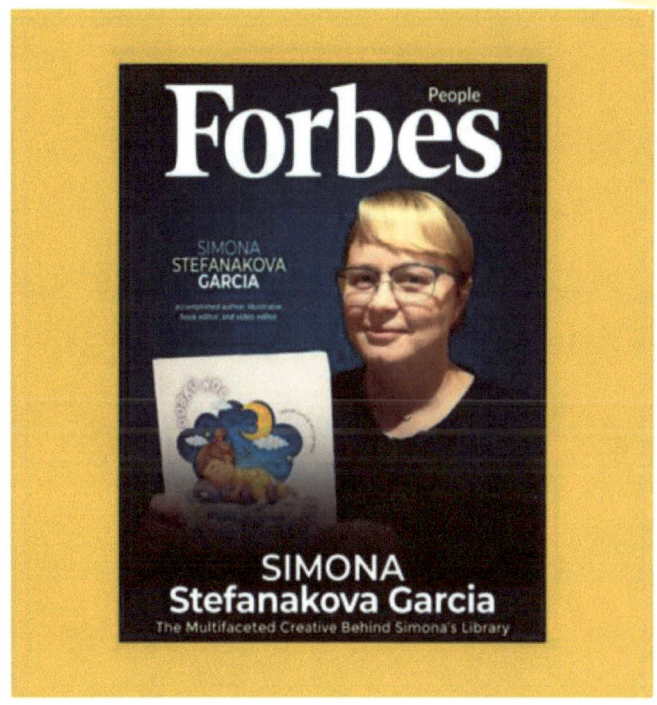